Miles V. Lynk

The black Troopers

or, The daring Heroism of the Negro Soldiers in the Spanish-American War

Miles V. Lynk

The black Troopers
or, The daring Heroism of the Negro Soldiers in the Spanish-American War

ISBN/EAN: 9783337133061

Printed in Europe, USA, Canada, Australia, Japan

Cover: Foto ©ninafisch / pixelio.de

More available books at **www.hansebooks.com**

The Black Troopers,

OR
THE DARING HEROISM
OF
THE NEGRO SOLDIERS
IN THE
SPANISH-AMERICAN WAR.

PROFUSELY ILLUSTRATED,

BY

MILES V. LYNK, M. D.,

Author of "The Afro-American School Speaker and Gems of Literature," etc.

Published by
THE M. V. LYNK PUBLISHING HOUSE,
JACKSON, TENN.

Dedication

TO THE MULTITUDE

OF PAINSTAKING AND CONSCIENTIOUS PARENTS,

IN WHOSE HOMES,

AROUND WHOSE HEARTH-STONES,

AND UNDER WHOSE TENDER, FOSTERING CARE,

THE GALLANT NEGRO SOLDIERS,

WHO DID YOEMAN SERVICE,

IN THE SPANISH-AMERICAN WAR,

TO THE THOUSANDS

OF BRAVE NEGRO BLUE JACKETS ENGAGED,

AND FINALLY,

TO THAT UNDAUNTED SPIRIT OF MANLY

VALOR AND HEROISM

THAT IS BOUND TO LEAVE ITS IMPRINT UPON

THE SHINING PAGES OF THE

WORLDS HISTORY,

THIS VOLUME IS RESPECTFULLY

DEDICATED

By the Author.

PREFACE.

HISTORY abounds in striking narratives of chivalry and heroism, of profound statesmanship and bitter national struggles; but its most glowing pages are those that record the proud achievements of patriotic soldiers and sailors, in their efforts for the supremacy. Sparta had her Thermopylæ, Haiti her L'Ouverture and Dessalines. Scotland had her Bannockburn, and immortal Bruce. The Afro-Americans have legions, who have forever immortalized themselves by their soldierly conduct in defense of human liberty.

It was with the desire to permanently write the names of these illustrious heroes upon the pages of recorded history, and thus insure to generations, yet un-born, a proud heritage, the writing of this volume, as incomplete as it may be, was undertaken. Having impressed my readers with the bravery, valient heroism, and true soldierly bearing of Afro-Americans as proven on recent battlefields, in camps, and as commissiond officers of the U. S., the consumation of a high ambition will have been effected. The status of Nations and Races is measured by thier industry, scholarship and bravery.

Considering all things, the Negro is standing the test as measured by these standards. Methinks I can see the day, just beyond the horizon of the blackening clouds, when the world, moved by the inexorable facts of plain history, will accord to the Negro all the considerations vouchsafed to the most favored branch of the human family. If not, why not?

On account of the scarcity of special correspondents with the colored soldiers in Cuba, we have made liberal use of the pages of the following papers for which we extend thanks, viz:—

THE FREEMAN, AGE, CHRISTIAN RECORDER, STATESMAN, NATIONAL STANDARD ENTERPRISE and PLANET.

Miles V Lynk,
Jackson, Tenn.

April 15, 1899,

The United States Battleship Maine,
before blown up

The United States Battleship Maine being blown up in Havana Harbor, Feb. 15 1898. Over 260 American sailors were killed, 24 of whom were colored.

PART I.

CHAPTER I.
INTRODUCTORY.

FOR convenience of studying the subjects herein treated, this book is divided into two parts.

Part 1st. is devoted to the history of the colored soldiers, enlisted in the regular army of the U. S. who took part in the Spanish-American war.

Part 2nd. gives account of the colored soldiers, who enlisted in the U. S. army as volunteers and not as regulars. Some of these volunteers saw service; others were prevented from relizing their highest ambition by the short duration of the war. Both regulars and volunteers, those who saw actual service and those who didn't, were equally heroic, and thus deserving of praise. One went into service when his time came and the other was prevented by circumstances over which he had no control.

CHAPTER II.
Causes Leading up to the War.

THE cause which gave rise to the Spanish-American War may be divided into two classes, viz:—Remote and Immediate.

Remote Cause.

One only has to study the colonial policy of Spain, extending through centuries, to notice the oppression, the curtailment of human rights and liberties, and the constant stream of bloodshed, consequent therefrom, to see the underlying causes that might give rise to a war of liberation. Cuba is situated right in the door of the U. S., so to speak. For centuries the Island had been a hot-bed of oppression. Spain had taken advantage of every opportunity to enrich her home treasury, at the expense of the Island colonists. There was no popular government. The people becoming tired of the tyranical yoke, made several attempts to gain their independence, notable among these, the bitter Ten Years War which began Oct. 10, 1869 and lasted ten years; and the war which had for its culmination the throwing off of the yoke of Spain. It began in April, 1895 and ended in Aug., 1898. Aside from the natural tendency of the U. S., to sympathize with a race of people, struggling for independence, these insurrections, over which Spain seemed to have little control, did much to interfere with American commerce and American property on the island.

For this and for humanitarian reasons, the American people, through their newspapers and through their representatives in Congress, demanded that the U. S., interfere to the end that Spanish rule should cease in Cuba.

Spaniards became very defiant of what they termed American interference in their affairs. Americans were offered many indignities on the streets of Havana, threats were made against American consular and other officers. But the American war spirit was not fully aroused until the U. S. Battleship, "Maine," was blown up in Havana Harbor on the evening of Feb. 15, 1898. This brings us to the

IMMEDIATE CAUSE.

It was supposed that the Maine, a second class battleship, and one of the best vessels of her class, was destroyed through Spanish treachery. Owing to the intense excitement, and the un-trustworthiness of the peasons who were competent to testify, this theory could not be proven. However, public sentiment in America favored it and all the administration, at Washington, could not prevent a declaration of war by Congress. Accordingly, Congress ordered intervention, Tuesday, April, 19, 1898.

Colored Men on the Maine.

There were thirty colored men in the crew of the illfated battleship Maine. This tends to further prove, that, notwithstanding the fact, white historians fail to give the Negro proper credit, yet, without his ever presence, American history would be void of some of its most illustrious pages. But we digress: of the thirty colored men on the Maine twenty-two were killed, and injured.

The following lost their lives, as the direct result of the explosion, to wit:— Geo. Johnson, Washington, D. C.; John T. Adams, Washington, D. C.; Daniel

Lewis, Washington, D. C.; Noble T. Mudd, Washington, D. C.; Chas. Anderson, Norfolk, Va.; Jas. Gordon, Portsmouth, Va.; William Lambert, Hampton, Va.; Robt. Perry, Norfolk, Va.; Alfred Simmons, Portsmouth, Va.; John R. Bue; William Coleman, Brooklyn, N. Y.; Charles Hassell, Salla. W. I.; Harry Jackson, Los Angeles, Cal.; Chas. F. Just, Charlston, S. C.; James W. London, Keyport, N. J.; John E. Marshall, Harrison, Ky.; John Mose, Rainwood, N. C.; James Pinkney, Annapolis Md.; John Warren, Randolph, S. C. William Coleman, New York, N. Y.; and two others.

The injured were: James W. Allen, Norfolk, Va.; Robt. Hutching, New York, N. Y.; James Williams, New York, N. Y. Henry Williams, Richmond, Va.

The uninjured were: Westmore James, Charles City, Va.; Daniel G. Toppins, New York, N. Y.; John Toppin, Long Branch, N. Y.; Alonza Willis, Keyport, N. J.;

CHAPTER III.
Negro Soldiers enlisted in the regular U. S. Army.

FOUR Negro regiments constitute the quota of troops in the regular U. S. army. They are the 9th. and 10th. cavalry; and the 24th and 25th. infantry. Before the breaking out of the war, they were stationed as follows. The 24th. regiment at Fort Douglass, near Salt Lake City; the 25th. at Missoula, Mont.; the 9th cavalry in the department of the Platt; and the 10th at Assiniboine Mont.

All of the commissioned officers of these regiments are white. The regiments were recruited in the 60's and are composed of some of the best disciplined troops of the U. S. Army. All of these veterans saw service in the Spanish-American War.

In the city of New Orleans, in 1866, two thousand two hundred and sixty six ex-slaves were recruited for service. None but the largest and blackest Negroes were accepted. From them were formed the Twenty-fourth and Twenty-fifth infan-

The First Spanish Prisoners of the War, being guarded by Negro Soldier at Fort McPherson, Atlanta, Georgia.

try, and the Ninth and Tenth cavalry. All four are famous fighting regiments, yet the two cavalry commands have earned the proudest distinction. While the record of the Ninth cavalry, in its thirty-two years of service in the Indian wars, in the military history of the border, stands without a peer; and is, without exception, the most famous fighting regiment in the United States service.]

Just before the actual declaration of hostilities, the NEW YORK TRIBUNE, among other things, had the following to say:—"Since 1862 the nation has had ample opportunity to test the value of the colored American as a soldier in a variety of ways on the battlefield, in the protracted siege, in Indian warfare, and in the trying service of preserving order and protecting life and property in the time of the great strike of 1894. During the closing period of the war he won for himself a place in the military world which he has been able to hold ever since. Fourteen colored soldiers received medals for heroic conduct during the short period that they served in the civil war; since then seven have won congressional medals for distinguished gallantry in action against Indians and robbers, and two have received certificates of merit in token of recognition of acts of special though less conspicuous bravery.

Physically the colored soldier is the equal of any boy, all talk to the contrary notwithstanding. The average height of the native white recruit is 67.76. inches. But in weight the colored man has decidedly the advantage. Of the recruits received between the ages of twenty-five and twenty-nine years, the average weight of the native whites was 146.25 pounds; the foreign born whites, 147.16 pounds, while that of the colored men was 149.42 pounds. In mere avoirdupois the colored soldiers lead the army, and in physical endurance they have proved themselves as tough as the toughest. This paper is also authority for following extract from the Surgeon's report on the subject of alcoholism among the Negro troops.

"The admission rate for alcoholism, was 29.06 for the army as a whole—31 20 among the white and 5 70 among the colored troops. Seven deaths among whites were due directly to this cause.

This is a slight improvement upon the record of 1895 which showed 30.11 as for the army, with 32.16 and 6.47 for the white and colored respectively, and a very considerable improvement on the record of the preceding decade, which gives 41.04 as the average annual rate for the army—4.62 for the colored and 45.07 for the white troops."

It further says:—

"The colored soldiers acquire the drill and readily take a fair degree of pride in it and are good shots. The colored regiments have done as well with the new rifle as any, the 25th. regiment leading the department in which it is located. That colored soldiers do not lack courage has been proven again and again. Gen. Merritt especially characterized them as 'brave in battle.'"

CHAPTER IV.
The 9th. Cavalry.

THIS regiment has done more desperate work in its time than any other in the service. The Ninth is no parade command. It was never given anything but a fighting assignment. It was never assigned even for a season at any of the desirable Eastern posts. This was not because they are Negroes, but because they are first-class fighting men.

Six months after the Ninth enlisted it received its first shock of battle. It was in the spring of 1867, at Ft. Lancaster, a small post on the Texas plains. The thousands of Indians who surrounded the fort made much sport of the black troops. The day they met them in battle their opinion changed. The Negroes fought like demons. They obeyed their white officers perfectly, and were more ready to fight than eat. An account of their conflict reached civilization several months later and was a revelation to those who had ridiculed the Negro as soldier. From that day it has been one long fight with the Ninth. Their deeds of daring would fill volumes, and, though their ranks have almost wholly changed since the first enlistment, the command has always been made up of fighters.

The Ninth remained on the Mexican border until 1875, enduring the horrors of Indian wars almost constantly. Then they moved into New Mexico, with headquarters at Santa Fe. There they continued to see hot service until 1881, when they went further north, with headquarters at Ft. Riley, Kas. Col. Edward Hatch was the original commander of the Ninth. He never faltered in his opinion of his black soldiers, and was with them in all their hottest work. Why, those Ninth cavalrymen would have followed Hatch to the devil, and though he had been in his grave these ten years, the memory of the gallant fellow continues to stimulate the dusky troopers he led against odds of ten to one among the reds of the Southern plains.

A HUNDRED MILES A DAY.

From Riley the Ninth continued north being transferred to Ft. McKinney Wyo. in 1895. The 1,400 miles the Ninth made overland just to show what they could do. And it was wonderful what time these men could make. No wonder they were a terror to the Indians, for they were here one day and 100 miles away the next, fighting like devils. The Government always kept these troopers in action and as the Indians moved further into the heart of the Rockies of the north, so were the troopers removed into more isolated district. They have remained in the North since 1885, being transferred, however, to Ft. Robinson as headquarters in the meantime.

Said a well known army man:—

"I recall a hundred desperate engagements of this troop, showing their wonderful coolness and daring qualities. Their hardest work in the Sioux campaign of 1890-91 marked the Ninth as a fighting command of wonderful energy. They were in the Bad Lands hunting Indains, 114 miles from Pine Ridge, on December 30, 1890. That was the day of the battle of Wounded Knee, where Custer's old command the Seventh, wiped out old Two Strikes's band of Sioux. Incidentally, it may be mentioned that the Seventh lost nearly two score of men there, so it was hot work on both sides.

That day the Ninth was instructed to get back to the agency as quick as possible. Guy V. Henry was then major of the Ninth. He is now Colonel of the Tenth, and Perry is Colonel of the Ninth. The Ninth rode to the agency, 100 miles away, in twenty-five hours; then without getting out of their saddles rushed off fourteen miles to the rescue of the Seventh Cavalry, which was threatened with total extinction at the battle of the mission. If the fighting Ninth had been an hour later Custer's old command would have suffered the same fate as their chief and his men did on the Little Big Horn. The Ninth faced the Indains after that terrible ride without slacking speed. The Indains recognized the regiment as it came over the hill north of the mission buildings and refused to stand their terrible charge, but scampered off in a hurry."

One of the most notable achievements of the Ninth Cavalry, and in fact one of the most extraordinary incidents in the history of the operations in the Indian country, was the dash of Troop D of the Ninth on October 3, 1879, at Milk River, when they went to rescue Thornburg's command, which was hemmed in by hostile White River Utes. Troop D was sent through the lines of the Indians with a hurrah. Every horse in the troop was killed, not one getting inside the brestworks. Yet, remarkable to relate, not one member of the detachment was killed. They ride like centaurs, and can shoot a revolver with each hand, holding their bridle reins in their teeth while their horses are running.

CHAPTER V.

The 9th's. Cuban Campaign.

WHEN war with Spain was declared it was in keeping with the eternal fitness of things that the 9th. U. S. Cavalry should be given a place of greatest danger—and consequently of greastest honor.

Accordingly, this regiment, popularly known as the "Black Buffaloes," was with the first division of troops sent to Cuba. This division was under the command of Maj. Gen. Shafter. The 9th. was in the brigade commanded by Brig. Gen. "Joe" Wheeler, an ex-confederate commander of cavalry.

The Rough Riders Ambuscaded.

"The Rough Riders" a New York cavalry regiment of whites popularly so called because it was composed of athletes and cow-boys, was with the division in which th 9th. was serving. This regiment was considered the crack, white volunteer regiment, and was in charge of Lieut. Col.

Theodore Roosevelt. These new recruits, not being used to geurrilla warfare, were ambuscaded by a handful of Spanish sharp shooters, and would have been exterminated had it not been for the timely arrival and quick work of the 9th. and 10th. cavalries. The following poem, by W. F. Powell, a white man is a monument, more enduring than granite, that shall forever stand as a Gibralter to the sparten courage of the Negro soldier around San Juan Hill and their work in saving the Rough Riders at Guasimas.

    Hark! O'er the drowsy trooper's dream,
    There comes a martial metal's scream,
        That startles one and all!
    It is the word, to wake, to die!
    To hear the foeman's fierce defy!
    To fling the column's battle-cry!
        The "boots and saddles" call.

    The shimmering steel, the glow of morn,
    The rally-call of battle-horn,
    Proclaim a day of courage, born
        For better or for all.
    Above the pictured tentage white,
    Above the weapons glittering bright,
    The day God casts a golden light
        Across San Juan Hill.

    "Forward Forward" comes the cry,
    As stalwart columns, and ing by,
    Stride over the graves that waiting lie
        Undug in mother earth!

Their goal, the flag of fierce Castile
Above her serried ranks of steel,
Insensate to the cannon's peal
    That gives the battle birth.

As brawn as black—a fearless foe,
Grave, grim and grand, they onward go,
    To conquer or to die!
The rule of right; the march of might;
A dusky host from darker night
Responsive to the morning light,
    To work the martial will!
And o'er the trench and trembling earth,
The morn that gives the battle birth
    Is on San Juan Hill

Hark! sounds again the bugle—call
Let ring the rifle over all,
To shriek above the battle poll
    The war god's jubilee!
Their's were bondman, low and long;
Their's once weak against the strong;
Their's, to strike and stay the wrong,
    That strangers might be free!

And on, and on for weal or woe,
The tawny faces grimmer grow,
That bade no mercy to a foe
    That pities but to kill,
"Close up!" "Close up!" is heard, and said,
And yet the rain of steal and lead
Still leaves a livid trail of red
    Upon San Juan Hill!

"Charge!" "Charge"! The bugle peals again;
Tis life or death for Roosevelt's men!—
    The mausers make reply!
Aye! speachless are those awarthy sons,
Save for the clamor of the guns—
    Their only battle-cry!

THE BLACK TROOPERS.

The lowly stain upon each face,
The taunt still fresh of prouder race,
But speeds the step that springs apace;
    To succor or to die!

With rifles hot— to waist-baud nude;
The brawn beside the pampered dude:
The cow-boy king—one grave—and rude—
    To shelter him who falls!
One breast—and bare—how'er begot;
The low, the high—one common lot;
The world's distinction all forgot
    When freedom's bugal callat

No faltering stept, no fitful start;
None seeking less than all his part;
One watchword springing from each heart,
    Yet on, and onward still!
The sullen sound of tramp and tread;
Abe Lincoln's flag still overhead;
They followed where the angels lead
    The way, up San Juan Hill!

And where the life stream ebbs and flows.
And stains the track of trenchant blows
    That met no meaner steel,
The bated breath— the battle yell—
The turf in slippery crimson, tell
Where Castile's proudest colors fell
    With wounds that never heald!

Where every trooper found a wreath
Of glory for his sabre sheath;
    And earned the laurels well;
With feet to field and face to foe,
In lines of bartle lying low,
    The sable soldiers fell!

And where the black and brawny breast
Gave up its all—life's richest, best,
To find the tomb's eternal rest
    A dream of freedom still!

A groundless creed was swept away,
With brand of "coward"—a time-worn say
And he blazed the path a better way
    Up the side of San Juan Hill!
For black or white, on the scroll of fame,
The blood of the hero dies the same;
    And ever, ever will!

Sleep, trooper sleep; thy sable brow,
Amid the living laurel now
    Is wound in wreaths of fame!
Nor need the graven granite stone,
To tell of garlands all thine own—
    To hold a soldier's name!

CHAPTER VI.
The 10th. Cavalry.

THESE stalwart boys of Uncle Sam's fighting family were with the 9th. at La Quasima, El Caney, and San Juan Hill. Col. Guy V. Henry was the commanding colonel. Its men are especially noted for their fine physical devejopement and stately carriage.

Their conduct around Santiago often called forth the loudest praise, even from the enemy. The day after the taking of San Juan Hill, says John. A. Ratham to the San Francisco Chronicle, a Spanish officer remarked to an American officer: "We knew the American soldiers would fight hard and bravely, but we didn't leave our positions, until we saw creeping on toward us these black men, these Haitians." "No not Haitians" said the American officer, "but Americans." What tribute to the bravery of the Haitian soldier! Spaniards did not retreat—not even from Americans, until they thought Haitians soldiers were in sight! Every race loving Negro's heart must swell within him while he reads these lines!

At La Quasima, where two of the Negro cavalry regiments arrived just in time to save the Rough Riders from being cut to pieces; at San Juan, where a Negro color sergeant was the first man to plant our banner on the top of the hill; on all the surrounding heights overlooking Santiago, and later among the sick and dying in the terrible fever camp at Sibony, where the Twenty-fourth Infantry had been placed to watch over and attend their comrade. it was always the same. The Negro from the beginning of the campaign to the end never for a moment showed anything but, the utmost devotion for the cause and a most reckless bravery and a stubborn courage. It was down at Siboney, that vile village that must always be associated in the minds of men who saw it after the battle of Santiago, with every-thing horrifying and sickening, that the great truth of the axiom "the bravest are the tenderest," was pertinent. These fellows had been seen scrambling up against the enemy only a few days before in the face of a withering and deadly fire, struggling on with clenched

Sergeant Horace W. Bivins,
10th United States Cavalry and Marks-man of the United States Army.

Major R. R. Wright,
Who was appointed pay-master in the United States Army, with rank of Major. He and Major John R. Lynch were the only two colored pay-masters appointed.

teeth and steady aim, and looking and acting like black demons let loose, and here in this little seaside village, though themselves exhausted with the labor of the two preceding weeks, they were nursing the wounded and tending the dying. Red Cross nurses were there too, but no woman acted more gently with her charges, or pressed the brow of sickness more tenderly than these same black soldiers. When they rode into the very jaws of death at La Quasima, to save the Rough Riders (White) from extermination, they must have presented a panaramic spectacle unequaled in the annals of military warefare. Well might the muses, with their souls running over with the fullness of poetical essence, say, (St. Joseph Radical):—

"When a rain of shot was falling, with a song upon his lips,
In the horror where such gallant lives went out in death's eclipse.
Face to face with Spanish bullets, on the slope of San Juan,
The Negro soldier showed himself another type of man.
Read the story of his courage, coldly, carelessly, who can—
The story of the Tenth at La Quasima!
We have heaped the Cuban soil above their bodies, black and white.
The strangely sorted comrades of that grand and glorious fight.

And many a fair-skinned volunteer goes whole
    and sound to-day,
For the succor of the colored troops, the battle
    records say;
And the fued is done forever, of the blue coat
    and the gray;
"All honor to the Tenth, at La Quasima."

CHAPTER VII.
Some Idividual Members of the 10th.

AFTER the roar of cannonry has ceased and the din of battle hushed, the real heroes of the conflict stand out prominently. Some operate the guns, others command, requiring great self-possion, nicity of judgement, and executive ability; still another class is given to tenderly care for the injured. It is the latter to which our hero belongs.

Never before in the history of the U. S. have Negro soldiers, of high rank, been given such an opportunity as in the Spanish-American war.

Dr. Auther M. Brown,

is one of the few Negro military surgeons, who stood out conspicuously for rare professionol skill. His life should be a stimulous to every aspiring Negro youth. He was born in Raleigh N. C., where he attended the public schools and thus fitted himself for the Freshman class of Lincoln University from which school he graduated in 1888. After his graduation at Lincoln, he immediately went to Ann Arbor, Michigan, where he entered the University of Michigan; here he persued his medical studies, delving deep into the mysteries of the Æsculapian idea for three years, graduating with high honors, in 1891. After plucking his M. D. degree he settled in Birmingham, Ala., practiced, and went into the drug business. Shortly after war was declared Dr. Brown organized a military company. It was not accepted, probaly from predjudice. He was determined, however to serve his country, and secured the appointment as an immune surgeon. He proceeded to Cuba at once, only to find that yellow fever had abated. He was appointed assistant surgeon of the 10th. cavalry, and has the proud distinction of being the only Negro surgeon to serve a regular regiment in Cuba. He was also the sole commander of the gallant Tenth, from Aug. 12, 1898 to Oct. 8, 1898, and during that time perfect peace and harmony reigned. He was in command when his famous regiment was reviewed in Washington by the president, immediately upon their return from Cuba.

Dr Auther M Brown, Assistant Surgeon of the 10th. Cavalry, the only Negro Surgeon in the regular army in Cuba

Serg't G. W. Berry, 10th. Cavalry, who planted the colors of the 3rd and 10th cavalries on San Juan amidst shot and shell. (Retired after 33 years service.)

His vim, untiring energy, discriminating judgement, irrepressible will power, together with his unassuming, dignified bearing, will certainly win him a high place in the future history of Afro-American military affairs.

Sergeant Horace W. Bivins,
is another member of the 10th. Cavalry who has made his mark, and who is destined to futher emblazon his name upon the gilded pages of history. He was born in Virginia May 9., 1862, and spent the first sixteen years of his life on his farther's farm. He attended night school, matriculated at Hampton Institute, Hampton Va., as a work student, and wound up his school career at Weyland Seminary at Washington, D. C. He joined the Tenth Cavalry June 10. 1888 and was immediately given a position as clerk in the adjutant's office.

His first record as a marksman was made in 1885, when he was proven to be one of the best shots in the army. He was promoted to corporal Dec. 15, 1891. He has won a great many prizes with the rifle. He performs the wonderful feat of letting a bird fly from each hand, then taking up a rifle in each hand and killing them in the order they were given their freedom. Sergeant Bivins won first prize in the regimental re-union, held at Ft. Custer, Mont. Oct., 1892. In august 1893 he won the first revolver silver medal for the best shot with the revolver. In 1894 he won the first gold medal with a score of 590 out of a possible 800 points, and three days later he distinguished himself by making the highest score with a revolver on competition that has ever been made in the army. He was then sent to the Department of Dakota to participate in the Army competition. There he met the finest marksmen in the United States Army; and here it was that he won, with ease, the first gold medal which entitled him to the first rank in marksmanship and the best shot in the army at the time. It was the record made in this memorable competition that caused Lieutenant M. H. Barnum to write, saying: "In the year of 1894 Sergeant Horace W. Bivins distinguished himself as the best rifle shot in the whole army and as one of the best pistol shots."

Sergeant Bivins was transferred to the "Distinguished Marksmen's Class" and was presented with the badge worn only

San Juan Block House, Showing Marks of Shots.

Fighting upon the crest of San Juan Hill

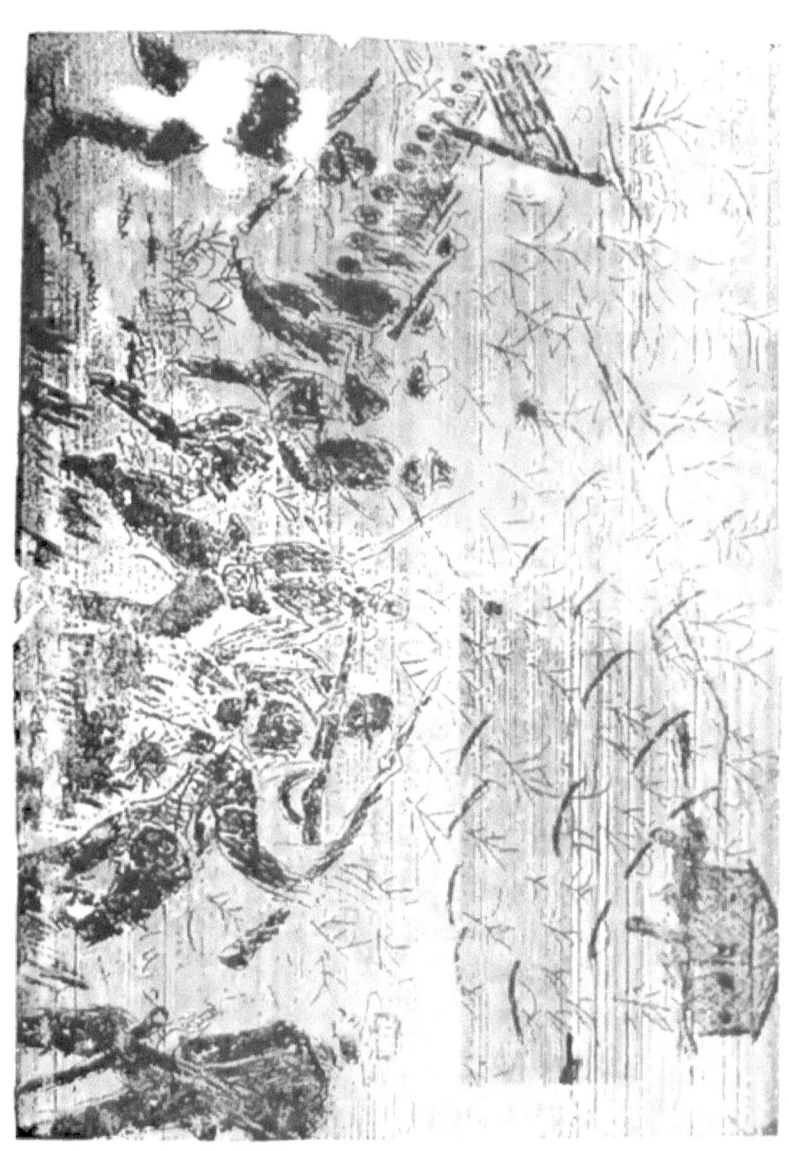

The charge of the 10th Cavalry up San Juan Hill

by members of that class, which badge bars him from every department competition except the one above mentioned.

Geo. F. Tyrrell

is one of the best musical directors in the U. S. Army. He is the leader of the band, composed of 25 artists, of the 10th. cavalry. Besides being a great Band Master, he is a composer of wonderful talent. His compositions are entrancing and exhilarating in the highest degree. Captain Tyrrell was born in England, at which time his father was in the English army, so you see he came of fighting stock. His future reputation as a soldier-musican is secure.

Private Robert J. Drake

is another member of the 'famous Tenth, whose history should cause every patirotic Negro's heart to feel proud. He is intelligent and highly educated; an athlete and orator of no mean ability. After enlisting with Troop G,. Tenth cavalry in 1898, he was held for special duty in the U. S.—a deserving compliment to his executive ability.

The following is a bit of reminiscences, told by 1st sergeant; James C. Williams, Troop M. 10th. cavalry, of their Cuban experience. It is a fine vindication of the

Negro's sticktoitiveness as a soldiers:—

"On the 8th day of June 1898 a small body of cavalrymen numbering 50 left Lakeland. Fla and proceeded to Port Tampa, Fla. where they embarked for Cuba on the Transport Florida and sailed to a point on the South western coast of the island of Cuba, after making a futle attempt to land at the mouth of San Juan river, they proceeded to Tunis where the transport ran aground. At this place a reconnoitering party of Cubans was sent out but they were ambushed by Spanish regulars and had one captain killed and 7 enlisted men wounded While stranded on this sand bar, the transport Florida was within the ranges of the Spanish battery and it seemed as if this little band of heroes were doomed to find a watery grave on the coast of Cuba when the Gunboat Helena hove into sight bringing joy to these heroes and destruction to the Spanish. Clearing themselves from the sand bar they were compelled to proceed to the south-western coast of the Island and there landing and joining General Gomez's army and marching into Santa Clara Province, they participated in the capture of El Hebro thereby capturing stores and munitions of war that were a Godsend to the starving Cuban army winning to themselve the admiration of the Commander-in-Chief of the Cuban forces

It was immediately after this fight that the command of this body of men known as Troop M 10th. Cavalry, devolved upon its 1st. Sergeant Lewis Smith, I think that this is the first instance in the history of our republic where a Negro has been placed in full command of the United States forces on foreign land. Sergeant Smith was born at Warrentown Virginia July 15, 1854. At the age of 21 he enlisted in Troop I U. S. Cavalry and has been Corporal Sergeant and 1st. Sergeant at various times since 1st enlistment. He has participated in numerous Indain campaigns against hostile Indians in the states of Texas, Arizona, Idaho, Indian Territory and other states. He led his troop into the fight of Royal Blanco last summer, Sergeant Smith had no assistance of any nature whatever from the United States. For more than two months he was cut off from all communication with the war department and for the last fifteen days on the Island had to subsist upon green corn, pumpkins, and alligators, they did not have salt to season these unsavory dishes with. After remaining on the Island for about three months they embarked for Montauk Point, New York, and arrived there Sept. 21st. 1898. The casualities of the trip was one man lost in Cuba.

CHAPTER VIII.

The 24th. Infantry.

THERE are many reasons why the 24th Infantry U. S. Regulars come in for special mention and praise for their conduct around Santiago. A captain of regulars, an board the transport with Rev. Astwood, A. M. E. Missionary, remarked: "We may blow all we want to, but the victory at San Juan belongs to the colored boys. I was there," he said, "and for my part, I would not be so mean as to rob them of it. When they dashed up the hill, the Rough Ribers and the 71st," he said, "were gone, our boys were beat, and but for the colored boys we would have been completely annihilated. They won the day." Thomas Bowles, of the Hospital corps, a white man from Herlford, North Carolina, said to him on the Sergurancia, "Rev. Astwood. I shall never forget the bravery of the colored soldiers." He said they were forging along the death angle, when a white comrade fell wounded. He was left by his company, and was calling in the agonies of death for help; they did not stop for him; just as he fell, two colored boys of the 24th, one wounded in the foot and one in the lung, hobbled by, stooped down and picked up thier white comrade and brought him to the rear. For this act he said," I will always stand by the colored man."

May he ever keep his vow! What Spartan

courage! What self sacrifice—they themselves at the point of death," yet forgot their own agonies to help a comrade! Words fail when I attempt to do justice to such brave soldiers. Verily, the Negro species furnish as great soldiers as the world has ever seen, or is likely to see in the future. It may be of interest to some to know the feelings of a soldier on going into the battle of San Juan, July 1, 1898, as told by J. W. Galaway of the 24th.

"Early on the afternoon of June 30, the day before the San Juan struggle, the rumor went the rounds of camp that the army was to move closer on to Santiago. The boys at once began to speculate on what was to happen as to the result of moving nearer the stronghold of the enemy; some ventured this and that and others grew apprehensive and could be seen soon after hurriedly penning a missive home as a probable last communication.

That my state of feeling was not that of fear, but suspense. I was not afraid to go into battle, but anxious as to the future; not scared, but anticipatory. I wondered as to the thoroughness of the preparation, whether we were ready to meet an enemy who had been preparing a defense before we thought of leaving our post on such a mission. This is somewhat how I felt on that afternoon and believe that this feeling was general thoughout the command. But the next day, what was that to bring?

The call sounded about 3:30 P. M., camp was broken and the whole Fith Army Corps was on the move. We were from half past three o' clock till nearly twelve that night going two and a half miles. It is but natural that on such a slow march one's mind runs to sea and dreams of what is to be. I confess that at times I became melancholy and apprehensive as to my fate, but it was not from fear. but suspense. I wanted the thing over with; wanted to go in and do what we had to do and be done with it, not to be dilly-dallying along, camping here and there. Fight we must and why not hurry with it, come what may? This is the feeling that hovered in the breasts of the ones who were to decide the fate of the Stars and Stripes. We went into camp on the night of June 30th the tiredest set of chaps I believe it possible to be gotten together.

The morning of July 1, awoke as pretty as I believe it possible for sunshine and

Trumpeter James Paine,
24th Infantry, who sounded the famous call that sent his regiment bouncing up San Juan like wild men.

blue azure to make it. Hurriedly we prepared our breakfast of hard tack and salt pork that we might be prepared when the call to "strike" camp was sounded, for I knew we had a task before us that day. I felt it, though no one spoke of our going into battle even if they knew that on that day we were to begin upon a work the conclusion of which no one knew. Why I was so melancholy, so sad and serious in mind and soul that morning, I have so often since tried to picture to myself the answer. But that the condition of feeling was one of extreme suspense only and only needed a sudden start upon the act in view to break it, (a feeling so often felt by those going on a journey who are impatient and anxious as to whether their train, or the hour at which it is due, will ever arrive.) At 6:10 A. M., when the first gun of Capron's battery sounded the opening peal of the battle, an entirely new feeling came over me; one of dare devil bravery, eager for the fray; willing to go into the fight and be shot down. In fact, I felt as though I loved the idea of being shot at. I had been held in a state of suspense as to when we were to try "conclusions" with the Dons and as to the face of the army of invasion; but now, relieved of that, I was anxious. I had been a witness to the fleet engagement with the land batteries on June 22, but now I was anxious to see men actually face each other, as I had so often seen in pictures and read about in descriptions of battles, etc., before I left home years ago to become a soldier.

Eight o'clock came; the brigade trumpeter came from his hive to express to us the command of the brigade commander. A few minutes later we had "struck" camp and were in the road on our way to the battlefield.

The battery guns above El Caney continued to boom! boom! with a human intelligence, appealing to the boys, telling them that they had begun the task that would try every inch of their souls to complete. The again we grew then indeed, for as we moved up the road we could hear the sharp, decisive ring of the musketry of those that had preceded us. Soon we met friends of other regiments wounded and being carried to the rear. The intense heat had caused a breathless silence to come over the ranks; the rattle of the tin cups against the scabbarded bayonet was more solemn than any funeral dirge I

Corp. Geo. Hutton, 24th. Infantry
Recommended for a commission as 2nd Lieutenant for bravery in the charge up San Juan Hill.

have ever heard; the colonel rode at the head of the column, solomn, serious and majestic. Everything seemed to aid in giving a deep sad impresion to the day. We all had vigorously cheered at the first sound of the cannon that morning, but now we were coming close to the scene of action no one seemed to dare open his mouth. Grimes' battery was just ahead, pouring at the enemy its most deadly contents and the noise it made as we came under it was enough to divide the strong from the weak. Here we disrobed, throwing off our blanket roll, etc., and only taking with us into the fight such as was necessary to life (if spared,) ration bag (haversack) and water can (canteen). we had now come to the real point of action, at place where a man is unable to describe the pulsations of his bosom; to decide whether he is frightened and afraid to do his duty, or posessed of bravery that leads him either to a command or a grave. With all the excitment and confusion of the day impressing itself upon me, I yet thought of my feelings. I had for two days nursed it, and now had come to stay; it would not be displaced, try hard as I might. The question whether I was a coward and afraid to do my duty haunted me; and was I equal to the occasion? Ah, suspense, to you was due all my agony of feeling in my first lessons of real war!

"Forward!" At the command my bosom swelled and all that was best in me came rushing forth. I have fought fright and cowardice and have won. An intense feeling of pride came over me, and bullets rained like hail and men fell everywhere. I was no longer afraid, and that evening, upon San Juan, I breathed a silent prayer that I had been a man and felt that I had done my duty fearlessly."

Two soldiers of the 24th, one wounded in the leg, the other in the lung, carrying a wounded white comrade to the rear.

Sergeant Major B. F. Sayre, who was noticed for "conspicuous bravery and coolness on the field of battle" at Santiago, and prom

CHAPTER IX.

The 24th. Continued.

THE 24th. AS YELLOW FEVER NURSES.

NOT alone in battle was the men of the 24th. extra serviceable, but when the scourge of yellow fever made its appearance in camp, when it was more dangerous to nurse the sick than to face Spanish bullets, they were not found wanting. Remember, there is no prophylaxis for yellow fever as there is for small-pox in the way of vaccination. The pest had made its appearance in camp, some one must nurse them. The call was made for 65 volunteer nurses. Who would answer, "Send me, send me." This work was considered more hazardous even than the sinking of the collier Merrimac at the mouth of the Santiago Bay by assistant naval constructor Hobson and his valient crew. Notwithstanding the staggering demand, 65 nurses from the 24th. Infantry readily volunteed for service. This was a crucial test of the metal of the men and an anxious moment indeed. From one company alone 15 gallant fellows responded and this fine example soon produced more than were needed for the purpose.

By the end of July yellow fever had over run all the hospitals, most of the 65 volunteer nurses, surgeons, cooks, etc., were patients. Still others from the ranks volunteered to go into the "Valley and Shadow of Death"—yea, death itself.

This was at Sibony, and it is a fact that, during the 40 days the 24th. was stationed there, not a murmer was heard from a single man. This is a glowing tribute to Negro soldiery. It shows his abilty as being able to turn from the field of strife and blood shed, to that of humanity, from that of killing to succoring the dying.

The 24th. Infantry, in its three days fighting, preceeding the truce, lost 98 officers and men killed and wounded, all but two of these being lost in the charge up San Juan Hill, July 1st. At one time 430 men were on the sick list-victims of the disease of the patients among whom they were working.

CHAPTER X

In The Trenches Before Santiago.

IT would tax the pen of a Frederick Douglas to correctly portray the hardships, or it would take the tongue of a Wendell Phillips to properly paint the extreme fortitude, which rose to the height of sublimity, experienced by the colored soldiers as they lay in the trenches before Santiago, from July 1st. to July 4th.— part of the time fighting, again in almost breathless suspense, while the rain "poured" and the heat almost as intense as if it were the fragments from Hades' blasts.

The following is a pen picture, drawn by Sergeant—Major B. F. Sayer of Co. C, himself noticed for "conspicous bravery and coolness on the field of battle" and accordingly promoted from the position of corporal of Co. C, to the post of Sergeant Major of the 24th. Infantry. Nothing thrills the souls of people more than a discription, by one who actualy participated in the engagement. With this ever view, and in order to lend authority to these accounts, the author has purposely included these personal reminiscences.

Sergt.-Major Sayer, in speaking of his experience, in the trenches, says, (New York Age;):—

"We broke camp on the morning of the 1st. The battle began at 5:30 A. M. between the advance army of Cubans and the Ninth Cavalry on one side and the Spaniards. We could plainly hear the sharp crackling of small arms and the roar and boom of the cannons as we were making our blanket rolls, and the thought that we were going straight to the front, and that, perhaps, this might be the last breakfast we should take on earth for many of us, sobered the most irrepressible.

We had to march in single file through a narrow mule path, shut in by dense woods and jungle on each side. As we drew near the firing line bullets began to hiss across the road, and a number of our men hit and a few killed without even seeing the foe or firing a shot in return. We passed a number of troops lying down behind trees and bushes as for shelter; but our order was to go to the front. The road led into a stream which was quite deep, the water reaching up to my arm pits. We waded this under a heavy fire and climbed the steep, slippery bank on the other side, cut the barbed wire fences (which are met with everywhere in this country) and found ourselves in a great field of grass, five or six feet tall, full of large trees. About half a mile across this field rose a high, steep hill (San Juan) with three block houses on the crest. It was from these and the intrenchments all along the top of this hill that the Spaniards were firing while the thick brush at the foot of it was lined with them, and nearly every tree that could afford concealment contained one or more sharpshooters. Our men charged right across with magnificent recklessness and daring and the Spaniards began to run. Right up the hill we went and they took to their heels, leaving their dead and wounded behind. We poured a fulisade of shots into them as they ran and dodged in the underbrush until they gained the shelter of their third line of entrenchment, about eight hundred yards away, just on the outskirts of the city, where they made a stand and fought us all that day till dark.

The battle was renewed before daybreak the next morning and continued without ceasing till 11 P. M. The next morning (Sunday) there was some little shooting but about noon this ceased and we were glad to get a chance to fortify our position, which is one of the best imaginable from a strategetic standpoint, and when the Spaniards lost it they were practicaly whipped. They fight strictly on the defensive from intrenchments and retreat from one to another when hard pressed.

They had prepared these defenses months before and they knew to a certainty the exact distance from one point to another. They are fair shots too and they had the advantage over us at first because they had us in view all the time and knew exactly how to sight their rifles. while for a long time we did not know where they were concealed; and then, too, thier sharpshooters in the trees were not discovered till after a number of our men and officers had been killed. The officers particularly had been singled out as targets and the loss among them was severe. The first day we lost over 1,500 killed and wounded. The enemy's loss must have been very great in the three days fighting, for our men buried over 500, and one can see bodies lying in the grass between us and them. The stench is almost unbearable."

It must have been sickening beyond description, as our soldiers occupied the trenches, as the Spaniards fell back—leaving hundreds of human carcasses, to furnish aroma for their respiratory apparatus, and this too, under the tropical sun and moist atmosphere of Cuba.

"Colored Soldiers in the Trenches before Santiago."

1

CHAPTER XI.
The 25th. Infantry.
How El Caney Was Won.

THE 25th. Regiment displayed remarkable bravery in the battle of El Caney. After all of their commissioned white officers were either killed or lay weltering in their life blood, and there was no one to command them, brave S. W. Taliaferro, (col.) 1st. Sergeant, Co. C. took command and led his company to victory. The following vivid description of that memorable conflict was given by M. W. Saddler 1st. Sergeant of company I himself a participant, in a communication to the New York Age:—

"On the morning of July 1, our regiment, after having slept in one part of the night with stones for pillows and heads resting in hands, arose at the dawn of day, without a morsel to eat, formed line, and after a half day of hard marching succeeded in reaching the bloody battle ground of El Caney. We were in the last brigade of our division. As we were marching up we met regiments of our comrades in white retreating from the Spanish stronghold. As we pressed forward all the reply that came from the retiring soldiers was: 'There is no use to advance futher! The Spaniards are entrenched and in blockhouses. You are running to sudden death.' But without a falter did our brave men continue to press on to the front.

In a few moments the desired position was reached. The first battalion of the Twenty fifth Infantry, composed of Companies C, D, G and H, was ordered to form the firing line in preference to other regiments, though their commanders were senior to ours. But no sooner was the command given than the execution began. A thousand yards distance to the north, lay the enemy, 2,000 strong, in intrenchments hewn out of solid stone. On each end of the breastwork were stone block houses. Our regiment numbered 507 men all told.

We advanced about 200 yards, under cover of jungles and ravins. Then came the trying moment. The clear battlefield was reached. The enemy began showering down on us volleys from their fortification and numberless sharpshooters and away in palm trees and others places of concealment. Our men began to fall, many of them never to rise again, but so sturdy was the advance and so effective was our fire, that the Spaniards became unnerved and began over shooting us. When they saw we were 'colored soldiers,' they knew their doom was sealed. They were afraid to put their heads above the brink of their intrenchment, for every time a head was raised there was one Spaniard less. The advance was continued untill we were within about 150 yards of the intrenchment, then came the solmn command, 'Charge.' Every man was up and rushing forward at headlong speed over the barbed wire and into the intrenchment, and the Twenty-fifth carried the much coveted position.

Our loses were as follows: Company A—wounded Sergeant Stephens H. Brown, Private William Clark. Company B—killed, Private French Payne; wounded, Private Thomas Brown. Company C—woundeed, Private Jos L Johnson, Samuel W. Holley, John H Boyd Company D—killed, Private Wm Howe, John B Phelps, John W Steele; wounded, Sergeant Hayden Richards, Privates

Robert Goodwin, Andrew Smith. Company E—wounded, Privates Hugh Swann, David Giiligin, John Sadler and James Howard. Company F—wounded, First Sergeant Frank Coleman, Private William Lafayette. Company G killed, Private Aron Leftwich; wounded, Privates Alvin Daniels, Benjamin Douglass, George P. Cooper and John Thomas. Company H—killed, Corporal Benjamin Cousins, Private Albert Strothers; wounded Henry Gilbert, William Bevels and Edward Foreman Officers—killed, Second Lieutenant H. L. McCorkle; wounded, Captain Eaton A. Edwards, Lieutenants Kennison and Murdock."

The personnel of the 25th. is remarkably good. The soldiers take great delight in the honors of their regiment—and by the way, military honors mean something.

"Remember the Maine" was the battle cry of the navy. The men of the 25th., however, led the army in their paraphrase of the chorus of "A hot time in the old town to night."

They termed it, which is as follows:—

HOT TIME IN CUBA SOME NIGHT

———o———

Since the Spaniards have tramped on our name,
Have starved 10,000 Cubans and blown up our ship, the Maine,
We'll dig them up in Cuba, and we'll not dig there in vain,
There'll be a hot time in Cuba some night

When we march into Havana with the Cubans on the run;
We'll show them quite a thing or two, Just how realfighting's done;

The Twenty fifth will lead the van, be first in all the fun;
And Spaniards will sizzle that night.

Spain has tried to fool with us, and make a little bluff,
When run against our navy, they'll be handled mighty rough.
But when they strike the Twenty-fifth they soon will have enough;
There'll be a hot time for Spaniards that night.

And they made it hot too.

HOW IT IS SUNG.

To get the full affect of the song, one has to hear it when the soldiers are lying around on the ground between 6 and 9 at night. Every man knows the words, and groups around, guitar and banjo players begin to sing. First one or two, then a second, and third, until the whole regiment is singing the tune.

If the Negro's voice is anything, it is musical. How entrancing must have been those strains of music as they pealed forth as if touched by the gods!

Before they sailed for Cuba, and while at Camp Boynton, Chicamauga Park, Ga., near Chattanooga, a white visitor, in speaking of the discipline of the 25th, said:—

"Battalion drill was held here yesterday afternoon. The companies were formed

Gallant charge of the 24th Infantry at El Caney.

Hotchkiss Battery,
(formed from the 1st, and 10th, Cavalry, white and colored respectively) in action at Los Guasimas.

In the Spanish Trenches around San Juan Block House.

in rank by the Captains and then marched up in front of Col. Burt's headquarters. The huge color bearer, and a colored giant of a private stepped forward, and halting, saluted. The regimental colors, a beautiful silk Stars and Stripes, with 'Twenty-fifth Infantry, U. S. A.' in blue letters on the reverse, in one of the white lines, was brought from the Colonel's tent. It was unfurled and the stiff breeze made it stand straight out. Waving it twice, the color bearer turned and marched across the field, guarded by the private. The band struck up the High School Cadets and the men resisted with difficulty the thrill of enthusiasm which made every private citizen on the ground raise his hat and cheer lustily.

'There's the kind of performance that makes patriotism,' said a bystander. 'It has done me more good than two dozen sermons.'

THE BATTALION DRILL.

He made similar comment when Col. Burt had the men in double file stretching across, perhaps, two city blocks. The gleaming of the setting sun made the dark faces look like bronze. Not a movement was noticeable until the command, 'Right

Shoulder Arm!" rang out, and the cotton-gloved hands passed over the blue coats and fell back again, as though some one was running the whole movement by pulling a string. For a well drilled regiment the boys from Montana can take rank with the best in the army."

PART II.

VOLUNTEER SOLDIERS

CHAPTER XII.
Volunteer Soldiers.

THE Negro has fought for the elevation and maintainance of the Stars and Stripes for centuries, in fact as long as any other inhabitant of the American Continent. It was he who first shed his blood for the first American Independence; It was he who turned the tide of battle at New Orleans; and his unbending courage and indefatigable work saved the Union, freed the Slaves, and forever saved the South from a condition of industrial and commercial stagnation, by throwing its owners, the white man, upon his own resources. Who can say that the Union could have been preserved had not over 150,000 brave Negro soldiers been enlisted in its cause?

The Negro's Valor Proven.

The Negro had proven a decided success as a soldier, not only in the defense of America, but elsewhere. Negro officers as well as soldiers, had shared the perils and glories of the campaigns of Napoleon Bonaparte; and even the Royal Guard at the Court of Imperial France had been mounted with black soldiers.

In three wars on the American Continent, the Negro's military ability had won the admiration and respect, not only of Americans, but Britishers—for they had a battilion of blacks, from San Domingo, in the battle of New Orleans—Not only Britishers, but of the world. for did not L'Ouverture and Dessalines put to route; even Napoleon?

The Burning Question.

In veiw of these facts, and ever keeping in mind that the Negro had fulfilled all of the requirements of American military rule; the question of Negro soldiers being commanded by Negro commissioned officers became both pertinent and prominent. This agitation was carried on by almost the entire Negro Press. Foremost among these agitators was John Mitchell, Jr., of the Richmond Planet.

His motto was "No officers no fight." He did not mean that the Negro was not loyal to his country but that, the man who had rendered valuable services in

The Haitian Flag.

Made famous because the Spaniards did not retreat until they thought their foes were black Haitians of whose citizenship this flag is the emblem. The top stripe is blue, the bottom red.

the defense of his country, from the Revolution untill now should not be debarred from wearing shoulder straps simply on account his color. The Negro's loyalty has been proven upon an hundred battlefield— the cry of their blood from the besmeared eminences of Bunker Hill to the beleaguered city of Petersburg attested this fact. The war department, apparently out of respect to the predjudice of some Negro-hating Southern journals, was not in favor of Negro commissioned officers. and accordingly, appointed none.

In speaking of the Negro's promotion from the ranks, Mrs. Victora E. Matthews, after visiting the Regulars, at Camp Wickoff; writes the New York Age as follows:—

"Instead of stopping to wonder if the black soldier has done the nine hundred and ninety-nine things that a black soldier would have to do before being even considered by a prejudiced board as one fit to aspire for promotion, the situation should be viewed as it is. Some of the saddest stories that could be amagined fell from the lips of men hardly able to say three words without halting for breath, in New York hospitals, in camp, and at such places as

Hampton, Va. Many men, now dead, said to me that nothing but the hope to get home to tell some one of their own race what they had endured kept them alive during the awful voyage home; how officers whom they had sworn to follow had subjected them to needless hardship, and neglect.

I saw men who, if they were white would have been covered almost from head to feet with medals for gallantry, actually sob like children at the mere effort to recall the scenes through which they had passed. One man who had seen twenty-eight years in the service,—and who was one of the first who entered Richmond after its fall—his experience was terrible he could not talk.— ' People, words won't do! People, listen, Andersonville was nothing beside it.' His tears ran like rain down his sunken face. He is dead now.

There are many reasons why white officers don't want any of the black fighters elevated. Many reasons why a black man when applying for promotion is rigorously subjected to every inch of existing law regarding examination, while any white youngster from the rank or civil life, whose father may have a little prestige or pull with the powers that be, can be ap-

Ex-Lieutenant H. O. Flipper. First colored Graduate from West Point Military Academy. Now special Agent Dept. Justice and interpreter of Spanish and Mexican Languages.

pointed to positions as high as second lieutenancy over battle scarred, but black heroes! Is this right?—if it is let us be dumb and accept contempts and inhuman treatment with humbleness and other cowardly attributes. If it is not let a No!! be thundered forth so that the heads of the Nation will hear it.

White men know that black men have lost all faith in them when it comes to applying the principles of universal brotherhood to blackmen. They know that the day of white leadership over black men has passed. It is in the stage that the crushed snake is that will hold on to life, will lash the air vindictively until sundown, but die it must. The claim that the black people are white hero worshipers falls flat on even the most sentimental. There is no question in any unprejudiced mind as to the black man's fitness to lead. That is not the obstacle in the way of making an officer of him in the regular army. The world knows he can fight, but United States' army officers do not want to know that he can be a gentleman! The thing now agitating army circles is not that he will bring disgrace on the service by officers inefficiency not that, but the question is must a white officer treat a black officer as a gentleman? That is the Gibraltar barring his progress. For that reason men likely to be a source of humiliation to his black comrades are chosen to stand as examples of the aspiring men of the regiment. Men of refinement good breeding, and character, are kept down by a system as repulsive to the senses as is cowardly in principle. No service rendered by the government can level this barrier. The black soldiers are helpless. Nothing but the creation of a public sentiment that will hound color hating officers out of the service can open the door of promotion and fair dealing for them. Every man and woman who feels a spark of just pride in the fame of our intrepid fighters should help in forcing the war department to consider these things and in making the distinguished head of our government know that ten million people are thinking this way and in this way and in teaching the children, as did Hamilcar, young Hannibal, what their rights are, though the fathers submit now to oppression."

Believing it just that Negro officers should command Negro volunteers, several Negro soldiers mutined when white officers were about to be forced upon them; notable among these mutiners, were a company that was recruited at Mobile Ala., and the 6th. Va., which we shall hereinafter notice.

A few leading papers, at the North spoke favorably of commissioned Negro officers. I say a few, because the author must admit, with regret, that he does not believe the people of the U.S. have approached near enough that utopian mellennialism, that would induce them to treat their brother in black with equal fairness. At first the North and South seemed about equally divided.

The New York Evening Post said:—

"The idea of enlisting Negroes in the South for service in Cuba seems to be in favor among the whites.

The New Orleans Picayune says that it has been repeatedly established by experience that the Negroes of that section are much less subject to the fevers brought there from tropical countries than the whites, and, even when attacked by yellow fever, suffer less than do the whites; which it explains on the ground that they belong to a tropical race, and still retain the constitutional peculiarities which are common to their kind. It recalls that, when the Spaniards after they had discovered and conquered the new world, tried to make the native Indians dig gold out of the mines for them, so many died that it was found necessary to import Negroes from Africa, who proved able to stand the strain. The Picayune thinks that, if the tropical possessions of the Spaniards in either the East or West Indies, or both, are to be conquered and held by the United States, Negro troops will be of the utmost importance for that service; and it is of the opinion that a considerable proportion of the soldiers to be sent to the aid of Admiral Dewey ought to be Negro troops.

We observe that the New Orleans editor contemplates the officering of such black regiments by whites, and it seems to be the general feeling in the South, as is not unnatural. General Russel of North Carolina, however, has appointed colored men as officers of the colored regiment furnished by that State."

Governers to the Rescue.

Notwithstanding the war department was not favorably impressed with the idea of Negro officers for Negro regiments,

Several governers, and some of them Southerners at that, appointed full regimental officers, from colonel down, from the ranks of the Negro soldiers.

This was the first time, in the United States, that a full regiment had been put under command of Negro officers.

Notable among the Negro regiments commanded by Negro officers were the 8th. Ills.; 23rd. Kansas; 3rd. North Carolina; and 6th. Va.

Company L. 6th. Infantry Mass. Vol.

THE FIRST NEGRO CO. WITH NEGRO OFFICERS; AND THE ONLY ONE IN A WHITE REGIMENT, was Co. L. 6th. Mass. Infantry. It has been in the Massachusetts Militia since 1863, when Mass. sent two colored regiments of infantry and one of cavalry to the front. All of this Co's. officers are colored, and the regimental battilion, of which Co. L. forms a part, has a Negro battilion adjutant.

According to the Adjutant General's report, its record, in the State of Mass., previous to the war, was second to none of the eighty infantry companies in the service of the State.

Its officers were made up, largely, of College-bred men.

The Oldest Military Organization

Co. L. is the oldest military organization, among colored people, in the United States. Its organization dates back to 1782. when the Bucks of America was formed. It was once presented a flag by John Hancock, one of the signers of Declaration of Independence, which flag is now in the possession of the Mass. Historical Society.

The Co. was commanded by Capt. Wm. J. Williams; First Lieut., William Hubert Jackson; Second Lieut., Geo. W. Braxton.

CHAPTER XIII.

The 3rd North Carolina Infantry.

ONE of the best organized regiments, with colored commissioned officers, was the 3rd. N. C. The following is a brief sketch of some of its officers.

Col. James H. Young.

The efficient commander of the 3rd. N. C. was born a slave of Captain D. E. Young, of Henderson, Vance County, N. C. He attended the common schools and entered Shaw University, in October, 1874. He was office boy for Col. J. J. Young, collector of internal revenue eight years, was promoted to chief clerk, and cashier, and was removed by President Cleveland, in 1885. In 1886 he was made chief clerk to the register of deeds of Wake County, which office he held until Dec. 1888. In July, 1889 he was appointed special inspector of customs, by the late secretary, Mr. Windom, and was again removed by President Cleveland. He was appointed by President Harrison, Sept., 1890, collector of customs for the port of Wilmington, N. C. and re-appointed in

1891, but the United States' Senate adjurned without confirmation. In 1894 he was nominated and elected, by the Republicans, to the State Legislature, and again in 1896. He is, therefore, a well tried man in public affairs.

His military career, began, however, when he was appointed Major of "Russell's Black Battilion," April, 27, 1898. As a testimonial to his efficiency, as a military tactician, he was promoted and commissioned Colonel of the 3rd. N. C., regiment, volunteer Infantry, June, 23, 1898. His superior skill as a commander brought his regiment up to one of the best drilled in the volunteer service of the United States;

Lieut. Col. C. S. L. A. Taylor

was born at Charlotte, N. C., January 31, 1854. He was born a slave, and a shoemaker by trade. He made shoes for General Lee's army during the late rebellion. Immediately after the close of the war he attended a Quaker school, and learned rapidly. He was prominent in Odd Fellow circles. before enlisting in the army—Ex Department District Master of Grant Lodge No. 7. P. M. V. P., Ex-Department G.C. of the I. O. G. S. and D.

of S. He was married in 1869 to Mrs. Agusta Wheeler of Charlotte, N. C. His entire family seem inclined to Military life—having two sons in the famous 10th. Cavalry. J. L. Taylor was sergeant of the 10th. Cavalry and was wounded in the battle of Santiago. George is also a sergeant. Lieut. Col. Taylor was a barber, musician, and dancing master, and had the reputation of having taught many of the first families of North and South Carolina how to trip the light fantastic. He was appointed first lieutenant of the Charlotte Light Infantry, Company B., in 1887, and was, after one year, commissioned captain, and commanded the Co. until April. 27, 1898 when he was appointed captain of Co. A., First Battilion, N. C. volunteers. He was promoted Lieut. Col of the 3rd regiment. N. C. volunteers, June 23rd. 1898. He was very popular with the regiment, and no man was more anxious than he to meet the "Dons."

Maj. Andrew James Walker was another popular officer with the regiment. He was commander of the first battilion: was born in Wilmington N. C. of slave parents. After the Civil War he attended the public schools. He was married in January, 1882 to Mis. F. W. Steward. Three children bless their union, one of whom was a volunteer in the regiment. He was appointed first Lieut. Co. B. 3rd. regiment, N. C. volunteers, April 26th. 1898 and was promoted to the position of major, June 23rd. 1898. Before enlistment in the army, he was an ardent S. S. worker and was for seven years elected president of the North Carolina Cape Fear Sunday School Convention.

Maj. J. E. Dellinger was born near Lowesville, Lincoln Co., N. C. At fifteen years of age he entered an academy near Lincolnton, in his native county, where, after three years study, he finished the prescribed course. After teaching for a while he took a course at the State Normal School, graduating at the head of his class, and winning the medal awarded the best scholar of the year's class. Next he became principle of the Reidsville graded school, and assistant principle of the Salisbury. He entered Leonard Medical school and graduated therefrom in 1892 with highest honors.

He was, on the 3rd. of July 1878, after

Capt. Wm. J. Williams, Co. L., 6th Mass. Vol. Infantry.

a competitive examination. appointed Chief Surgeon of the 3rd. N. C. regiment. He ranks as one of the best surgeons of this Country.

CHAPTER XIV.
The 8th. Illinois Infantry.

THE 8th. Illinois filled a very important position in the United States service, during the Spanish-American War. They were part of the army of occupation, and its commander, Col. Jno. R. Marshall, was military governer of the town of San Louis Cuba. The officers were as follows: Col. John R. Marshall; Lieut. Col. J. C. Johnson; Majs. Robert R. Jackson and Franklin A. Dennison; Adjutant, Harvey A. Thompson; Quartermaster, James S. Nelson, Chief Surgeon, Major Wesley. After forty days of waiting at Camp Tanner, they struck camp, and sailed for Cuba, on the transport cruiser, Yale, on the after-noon of Thursday, August 11th. 1898. Upon their arrival in Cuba, Chaplain Jordan Chavis wrote the National Standard Enterprise, under date of August 24th. as follows:—

"We had a very pleasant trip across the sea. A few were sick. I never experienced a finer trip and had my health

Col. James H. Young, 3rd North Carolina Vol. Infantry.

better than before. We reached Santiago Harbor the 16th. and landed the 17th. It was dark when we got ashore. We marched two miles from the city through the mud and struck camp. The next morning we moved back one mile and the second day thereafter were ordered to San Luis, the first battalion preceding us the day before. It was 2 o'clock A. M. when we reached here, so we remained on train until morning. Soldiers struck camp one mile from the city. We made staff headquarters in the city. We have good houses and everything is well if they will just let us stay here and I think they will. We have entire charge of the city and railroad, a distance of thirty-five miles. There are 6,000 inhabitants here. Everthing is oriental. Bull carts are used for hauling loads. The yoke is strapped to their heads by which they pull instead of their shoulders. From one to six pair are worked to one cart. Pack mules are also used extensively. Small ponies are used for riding.

Cows, goats and jennies are used for milk. It was a strange thing to see a boy peddling milk, ride a jennie up to a door, get down and milk from the jennie one-half cup of milk and ride to another door and do the same.

Plenty of men and women are around the streets, half naked, eating what they can gather from our camp.

There is great sickness and suffering among the Cubans.

Our regiment is having good health. Two companies left this morning for Palma Sarino, 12 miles from here, under Major Jackson, to take charge.

With proper care I think this is a healthy climate. The towns are filthy, but we are putting American enterpise into them and we will soon have a nice little city here."

As has been stated, Col. John R. Marshall acted as military governer of San Louis Cuba, a city about half the size of Springfield, Ill.

Major R. R. Jackson, with companies E and F, were stationed at El Paso, about 12 miles from San Louis; Major Jackson was acting Mayor of that town.

Thus it will be seen that these Negro soldiers were given responsible posts— posts calculated to show to the world that the Nergo is as able to command as he is to obey. And it should be said, here, that

Lieut Col. C. S. L. A. Taylor, 3rd North Carolina Vol. Infantry.

the Negro should be commanded by Negroes was amply justified. The return home of the 8th Illinois was one continual ovation, from New York to Chicago.

CHAPTER XV.
The 23rd. Kansas Volunteer Infantry.

THIS Regiment has the proud distinction of being one of the only two regiments, officered by Negro officers, that did garrison duty in Cuba.

A dramatic incident is told by Captain W. B. Roberts, of Co. F. of his experience at a Santiago hotel. Capt. Roberts, writing to his parents, Oct. 3rd, 1898 says:—

"When we are in Santiago we are reminded so much of home. There is a hotel there called the American, run by an American who is from St. Louis, Mo. They try to draw the color line here in Cuba. The first time I was there I went to that hotel along with Captain Hawkins, of Atchison, who is very light in color. They thought he was white and so said nothing to him, but the proprietor was going to stop me. He said his boarders and white customers objected to eating with colored men and that he could not afford to ruin his business by accommodating me, and I an American army officer in full

Colonel John R. Marshall,
8th. Illinois Volunteer Infantry

uniform; and you should have heard me go after him. I told him I was an American officer and had associated with gentlemen all my life and did not now propose to disgrace myself or my shoulder straps by eating at a side table or or in a side room to please a few second class white officers who never had money enough to take a meal at a first class hotel until they became officers in the volunteer army in the United States during this present war; that I asked no special priviliges, but would have what is due me as an army officer or know the reason why; that he need not think that we colored soldiers who spilled so much of precious blood on the brow of San Juan Hill that it might be possible for him and other Americans to safely do business, and are standing now with bayonets upon our guns as sentinels to protect them in that business, were going to stand any discrimination on account of our color; and all I wanted to know was whether or not he would feed me. The dining room was full of officers and others and you could have heard a pin fall while I was talking, and while the proprietor was finding something to say, an officer whom I later found to be

Gen. Ewers of military District No. 1, got up from the table, walked over to me grasping my hand, said: 'Come, Captain, take my seat; and you, Mr. Hotel Proprietor, get it quick; and I don't want to hear any more of this d—n foolishness with these officers of mine,' and I was a little king there in about a minute."

Captain Roberts never had any trouble with that hotel proprietor thereafter. While it is true that the Spaniards possessed many traits of cruelty yet they were more humane in many respects than the people of the U. S. The fact must inevitably accur to any well thinking man that their barbarities have been much exagerated. American liberty is often taken for license. Speaking of Spanish equality and fairness brings to my mind a little episode, which occurred in Havana; Feb. 1899. The associated Press Dispatches announced the following, under day of Feb. 14, 1899.

"Holman's Washington Cafe, in Central Park, has been ordered closed by Senor Frederico Mora, Civil Governer of Havana, because of the refusal of the proprietor to serve drinks to a mulatto, the Cuban General, Ducasse. Several friends of Ducasse were seated in the cafe taking re-

Lieutenant Colonel James H. Johnson,
8th. Illinois Volunteer Infautry.

Corp Wm H Farmer
8th Illinois Volunteer Infantry.

freshments, when he happened to be passing and they called him to join them. Mr. Holman, however, refused to serve him. As the existing Spanish laws prohibit race distinctions, Senor Mora, to whom complaint was made, consulted Maj. General Ludlow, Military Governer of the Department of Havana, as to the action to be taken. Gen. Ludlow told him to enforce the law, and Senor Mora informed Mr. Holman that unless he wrote a letter of apology the cafe would be closed. Mr. Holman declined to write the letter, and Senor Mora issued the closing order.

Mr. Holman, who is an American, says he will reopen, claiming that he is sustained by the American authorities. It is considered that the controversy will raise the race question."

Can it be possible that Spain, much abused, cruel Spain, would treat its citizens of color with more consideration than proud America— the land of the free and the home of the brave! It is a fact, however, that there had been much more equality among the races, in Cuba, under Spanish rule than in America. Think of it, Maceo, a Negro, yet second in command of the Cuban forces!

The 23rd Kansas did good service, on garrison duty in Cuba.

Capt. Roberts. writing from San Luis De Cuba, Sept., 7, 1898, Says:—

San Luis is the most peculiar city I have seen or dreamed of. It is situated in a beautiful valley between the Sierra Madre mountins, a unique Cuban town of about 4,000 inhabitants, all Cubans and colored people, but all speak Spanish and we cannot understand what they say, only a few words. "Man" in their language is "humbre," the "h" being silent; woman, "senora;" young lady, "senorito;" children, "pickaninnies," boy, "bache;" and a girl is called a "muchache."

We are camped on the outskirt of the town, just across the branch from the Eighth Illinois regiment, and have met several of the officers, and think a great deal of them. All are getting along nicely together. Our men visit back and forth and have a good time.

We have but little sickness in camp; most of what we have is bad colds and malaria. We have 24 men in the hospital, but none seriously sick. It is impossible to keep from taking cold until a person gets acclimated. It is very hot in this

The Cuban Flag, under which Maceo, Garcia, Gomez and other Cuban patriots fought. The stripes are blue and white and a white star in a red field.

Gen. Antonio Maceo.

climate and the nights are cool enough to sleep under blankets; and it rains every day. Big dews fall at night. So you see the weather conditions are much different to any thing we have been used to, but I am feeling fine, except a slight cold, and am trying to keep well

There is no yellow fevor here, but a good many cases in Santiago, there being there two hospitals for fever patients. This country is five hundred years behind ours. Little dirty streets, with houses worse than our barns, made of bark from cocoanut trees, which are the most common trees here. It is a sight to see our men climbing cocoanut trees after cocoanuts, some green, some about ripe. Will have ripe fruit here plenty in about two weeks. Everything grows here—lemons, oranges, pineapples, bananas and all tropical fruits. We have plenty of lemons for lemonade by picking them from the trees on the hillside anywhere around.

This is a great country of possibilities, but poverty reigns supreme. The fields are grown over with sod, and as wild as they ever were in the world. The people are pitiful sights, nearly naked and half starved, little bony boys, girls, women and men.

We have seen one Spanish soldier since our arrival, but evidence of war is everywhere—cannons, old Spanish ones, block houses or small forts, on every hill.

As I sit in my tent writing I can see two Spanish block houses within a quarter of a mile. The Spanish guns that were captured are being transferred to Santiago from where they will be shipped to the United States. I saw 20,000 Spanish Mauser rifles in a pile in Santiago when I was there the other day.

These people treat us as best they can, and do everything to make friends with us. Our regiment has about 200 Spanish mules grazing on the hillside near camp, which are in our charge, and our boys have a time riding these little mules around and getting kicked by them.

This is no place for women, because there is no place for them to stay; but if we were in Santiago or any other place of any size we could accomodate the ladies, and it may be possible soon for us to do so. As soon as possible we officers have a plan to bring our wives here, that they may see the country and people. It would be worth a fortune to anyone to be here for awhile and see what I am seeing.

Santiago has many fine palaces, the remains of Spanish aristocracy now occupied as offices by the officers of the American army.

There is some talk of sending us to Havana, but we don't know anything definitely about it, but I think it is a "black" dispatch, as there are all kinds of rumors here every day.

The barracks where the Eighth Illinois is quartered is an old Spanish prison and there are evidences of all kinds of cruelty and butchery—beheading blocks all covered with human hair and dried blood, and pieces of rope still hanging from the old round rafters, where many a poor unfortunate Cuban has been hanged. Old bloody blankets were carried out of that old crib of a barracks, where Cubans had been butchered, and burned by American soldiers. Some of these sights are terrible, while there is a great satisfaction in seeing the result of Spanish misrule and butchery.

It is reported that there are 1,500 Spanish soldiers in the hills about 65 miles from here and we may have a tie-up with them any time, as they have been ordered to come in and lay down their arms, but they have as yet, refused to do so. Gen. Ewers, our commander, has given them until the 20th to report in here and lay down their arms, and if they do not comply, we will have to go out and bring them in; and these 2,000 Negro troops here are the ones that can and will be pleased of the opportunity to do it. We hate the Spanish more and more every day we see the result of ten years war and confusion, for they have made a barren tract out of a once fertile field."

CHAPTER XVI.

The 6th, Va. Volunteer Infantry.

NOT a nobler set of valient hearted men ever enlisted in the miltary service of the United States. At the beginning of their enlistment strong pressure was brought to bear upon the governer of Virginia, to have them mustered in with white officers. This influence, mind you, came from Negro hating whites, who would rather see the Negro enjoying the congeniel(?) sunshine of Hades than see him in the regulation military uniform of the United States. It may be that they are conscious of the many indignities heaped upon the Negro by the so-called seperior race, and are cautious, lest he who sows the mind might reap the whirlwind.

Gen. U. S. Grant was once heard to remark that, "It will be a dark day when the Chinese learn the art of modern warfare." While the Negroes of this country have no desire whatever to turn their knowlidge of operating a machine gun upon the whites among whom they live, and many of whom they regard as their best friends; yet a faint idea, conspicious for its ineradicability, seemed to gain foothold in the minds of the powers that be, that a general arming of the Afro-American was inexpedient at least from their point of vantage.

History, from time immemorial goes to show that it has ever been the policy, with here and there an exception, of ruling races to keep military affairs out of the hands of subject races. The keeping in view of this idea and a knowledge on the part of the ruling class of this country of the ennobling of Negro manhood enevitably consequent upon Afro-Americans exercising the military prerogative, is what has prevented the promotion of Negroes in the army.

However, the blacks of Virginia, headed by the "gamest Negro editor on the Continent," John Mitchel, Jr., held out for Negro officers for the 6th. Va. While the Virginia Negroes were as patriotic as any other American citizen to be found elsewhere, he wanted simple justic, nothing more nor less. Therefore, their watchery was, "No officers, no fight."

The result was, Gov. Tyler of Virginia,

appointed all colored officers except a colonel, Lieut. Col., and an assistant surgeon.

The Colored officers

were; Majors, W. H. Johnson, of Petersburg; J. B. Johnson, of Richmond; Capts.; W. A. Hawkin, B. A. Graves, Charles B. Nicholas, Jas. C. Hill, J. A C. Stevens, E. W. Gould, and Peter Shepherd, Jr; Lieutenants, S. B. Randolph, Geo. T. Wright and David Worrell. Assistant Surgeon C. R. Alexander. All these officers were examined by the military board of Virginia before being commissioned.

Trouble For The 6th.

Lieutenant Col. Croxton (white) soon became tired of Negro officers, not withstanding their proven efficiency. Therefore he decided upon a plan by which he hoped to oust the Negro officers and have whites put in their places, namely to prefer charges of incompetence against the colored officers, have a prejudiced board appointed to examine them, and thus discharge them. This was about the middle of Oct., 1890.

A Distinction with a Difference.

In order to avoid the appearance of discriminating on account of color, Maj. J. B. Johnson, Capt. W. A. Hawkins and

Capt. B. A. Graves were not disturbed. Assistant Surgeon C. R. Alexander was not included, because the examination of him would have led to the examination of Assistant Surgeon Black, (white).

A List of the Victims.

The following however were marked for slaughter: Major W. H. Johnson, of Petersburg, Va; Capt. Charles B Nicholas, of Richmond; Capt. James C. Hill and Capt. J. A. C. Stevens, of Petersburg, Va.; Capt. Edward W. Gou'd and Capt. Peter Shepherd, Jr., of Norfolk; and Lieutenants S. B. Randolph, George T. Wright and David Worrell.

A Manly Act.

Knowing full well that no fair examination would be held, all of the nine officers ordered to be examined, promptly handed in their resignation to the War Department. After the question had been agitated in public prints, pro and con, the colored officers, who resigned, sent the following signed statement to Editor John Mitchell, Jr. of the Planet which appeared under date of Nov. 19, 1898:—

Editor John Mitchell;
Richmond PLANET;
Dear Sir:—As the daily papers generally

have given their supposed version of the resignation of the nine officers of the Sixth Virginia Volunteers and it has all been unfavorable to the officers in question, it may be well to let our friends hear our side.

To begin with, by an act of Congress the commanding officer of a regiment is allowed at any time he sees fit, to ask for a board to examine into the qualification, efficiency, conduct and capability of officers under him.

A Commanding Officer's Opportunity.

This of course gives a commanding officer an opportunity to get rid of any officer who may be objectionable to him, whether on account of color or any thing else. A West Pointer can have room made for his fellow school-mate to the detriment of the volunteer officers, and the colored officers can be gotten rid of for the volunteer officers of choice.

It is stated that we were incompetent. If West Point is to be taken as the standard of efficency we admit that we were incompetent, so is every one else, not a West Point graduate.

A Pointed Question.

Again, if we were incompetent, what is

to be said of any who are inferior to some of us resigned, in metal capacity? When we reason along this line, we can see that the object was not to find out our efficency etc., but to throw us out.

Had the Board met at the time appointed, we would have been summoned to appear before the Board not knowing what was wanted of us. The order called for a meeting of the Board on Monday, Oct. 3rd, at 10 A. M. We received the order from the Adjutant's office Monday Oct. 3rd, 9 P. M. Snap judgement.

Summary Proceedings.

We were not aware of anything of the kind to take place till we read the order. Tuesday, 7 A. M., some of our resignations were in the Adjutant's office. At 9 A. M. the President of the Board arrived in camp. We were sent for. While some of us were standing at the front of the commanding officer's tent waiting for the others to appear, we heard the question coming from within the closed tent "Are there any officers or men fit for promotion?" The reply was "No." In a few minutes the President of the Board came out and said to us, "The Board will convene Wednesday, 5th, at 9 A. M.

Major Wm. H. Johnson
6th. Virginia Volunteer Infantry.

Lieutenant John H. Alexander, (Deceased)
Second Colored Graduate from West Point.

A Significant Hint.

"If any of you wish to resign you had better do so before the Board meets. If your resignations are not in before we meet we'll have to report on you." Those words were significant. Why should he have said that?

The intention to get rid of colored officers was evident. We did not fear a fair examination as some of us had been examined more than once, and one of us three times, being always successful; but we were satisfied that it was a case of trot them out and knock them down.

The Military Board of Virginia

We consider that the officers composing the military board of the State of Virginia, Colonel Jno. Lane Stern, General Charles J. Anderson and other prominent gentlemen who examined us, or some of us at least, pronounced us qualified for our position, knew their business as well as the commanding officer of the Sixth Virginia Regiment, and their signatures to our papers are enough for us. The signatures of all the examining boards that could be established would not have added any more honor to, or attested to our qualification any more so than the names of these two officers above referred to. The Commonwealth of Virginia felt satisfied at their action, hence our entry into the service.

No Regimental Drill Held.

We can say without fear of successful contradicton that from the 9th of August, possibly from the establishment of the camp beyond Richmond, not one regimental drill had been had by the Sixth Virginia Volunteer up until the 22nd of October. saving a few maneuvers executed preparatory to a review by General Breckenridge on the next, neither had there been one officer's school of instruction other than those held in which the two Majors were instructors up to the 12th of October.

Performed Their Full Duty.

We did our duty, the regiment was complimented time and again upon its efficiency, yet after any drill, or at any time any shortcoming was noticed on part of enlisted men on the field, or sentinels at post, the officers were liable to be summoned to listen to a tirade of exercration and oaths. Oaths and curses were always on hand. They were often and very loud.

Friends Were Faithful

Our friends have stood up boldly for us,

and if our pretended friends could have witnessed the work done by the officers, and the assistance given us, and then seen what we had to contend against, instead of criticizing and condemning our action they would have commended us. Charity would have dictated that they say nothing until they heard more, but unfortunately for some of our people, the less they know about a subject the more they discuss it, and the discussion is rediculous, without sense or reason. We were there and knew.

A Word To The Critics.

These critics were at home and tried to know more than we and what they do not know about military regulations and usages would fill forty encyclopedias. We did just what the white officers of a Massachusetts Regiment did under the circumstances, barring color. We do not wish money at the expense of right treatment. One thing has been demonstrated, yea two, first, that the commanding officer of the 6th Virginia Regiment has no respects for a man of color, refined or vicious.

Colored Officers, Predicament.

All look alike to him. Second, that in the eyes of a certain class of army officers, an enlisted man, or an officer if he be a colored officer is no more than a yellow dog.

We do not wish it understood that we were utterly friendless. We were certain that we had one and probably two officers on the Board who would have given us justice, but one of the other officers was from a regiment very closely allied to the Georgia Regiment which gave us more trouble than all Camp Poland combined, while the other two, one of whom was the President, was from a regiment, the 4th Tennessee, who hated us intensely, as evinced by their action on learning that we were to be temporarily assigned to the same brigade with them. We had nothing to hope for. Only swift judgement.

Signed:

WM. H. JOHNSON,
J. A. C. STEVENS.
DAVID WORRELL,
JAMES E. HILL,
EDWARD W. GOULD,
C. B. NICHOLAS,
S. B. RANDOLPH.

A Lynching Tree Annihilated

A report, illustrating the character of the 6th. Virginia was related by a correspondent, namely; shortly after the regiment was moved from Camp Poland, Knoxville, Tenn., to Camp Haskell, Macon, Georgia, some one pointed out to them the tree on which a colored man had been lynched nine years ago, they proceeded to treat the tree as they would have treated the lynchers, and about a thousand shots tore their way through its trunk and cut away the limbs.

Kindling Wood In Abundance.

To complete the work axes were brought into play and the mighty monarch reduced to kindling wood. The white owner showed up on horse-back, but when he found that those Virginia colored folks were usually serious his horse's head was turned in another direction and for a few moments the boys enjoyed the sight of seeing his coat-tails play in the wind while his horse was made to do its best in getting him out of the neighborhood of danger.

The 6th. Reviewed by President McKinley.

While at Camp Haskell, Macon, Ga., the

otn. was reviewed by President McKinley, while on a Southern tour. A correspondent of the Planet writes as follows, under date of Dec. 1898:—

A Long March.

This morning reveille was sounded at 5:30, the boys were given breakfast 5:45 and everything put in readiness for the Grand Review given for our Corps Commander Maj. Gen'l Wilson in the city at nine o'clock. At 7 o'clock our command left camp for the long march to town, which was reached shortly after 8 o'clock. Every man was in heavy marching order, with his rifle, canteen, haversack with lunch, shelter tent, ponche and blanket rolled across from shoulder to waist. More than 7500 troops were in line, and it was truly a magnificent sight as they marched through the streets and passed the reviewing stand headed by the Division Commander and his staff mounted, followed by the 7th. Regiment of cavalry with their mounted band.

It was a sight never before witnessed by the citizens of Macon, and the idea of of 4000 Negro troops in line was something that they never even dreamed of before.

Favorably Commended.

The boys created considerable favorable comment however. It is strange how these people regard the Negro soldier. One cannot go into town without being eyed suspiciously, and looked upon as something out of the ordinary. this applies to colored as well as the white element. It is noticeable. so far different from the manner in which we were treated by all classes of citizens, while we were stationed at Knoxville.

CHAPTER XVII

The 10th. Georgia Volunteer Infantry and 9th. Ohio Battilion etc..

THE 10th. Georgia Regiment was a splendid set of soldiers, considerd from an athletic and disciplinary stand-point. The regiment was well behaved, gentlemanly, and would have shown the Spaniards a thing or two had not the fun ended so abruptly.

Company K

was recruited by Prof. Thos. L. Cotton of Darlington S. C. He was the only colored man in the regiment to recruit a company.

Company F

was one of the most inteligent companies in the regiment. It was from Hampton, Va., Capt. P. V. Turney, commanded. Capt. Turney was an old army man of 24 years constant service, and eminently fitted for his command.

Company A

was composed of men from Atlanta, the Gate city. Lieut. F. H. Crumbly was in

Lieutenant F H Crumbly.
10th Georgia Volunteer Infantry.

command. His men were well disciplined and had the highest respect for their Lieutenant.

Company G

was made up from volunteers from Augusta. Capt. Mullarky, Capt.; H. White, first Lieutenant.

Company B

was recruited at Richmond, Va., enrolled the 6th. of July, and mustered into service, July 6, 1898. Capt. Crandall Mackay of Washington, D. C. So you see this regiment was made up of companies from several states—all fine soldiers, however Rev. Richard Carroll, was chaplain and did good work, He distributed more than $300.00 worth of books, given by friends, among his regiment.

The 9th. Ohio Battilion.

The 9th. Ohio Battilion was also commanded by colored officers but due to the short duration of the war never saw service.

Major Charles Young, the commander was a West Pointer and his staff was composed of Senior Captain R. R. Rudd; Lieut. Wilson Ballard, adjutant; Captain Walter S. Thomas, quartermaster, Lieut. William Warren, asistant surgeon.

The officers of companies were Captain R. R. Rud, Lieut John R. Rud and William Elliot, of company A; Captain Deaton J. Brooks, Lieuts. Charles Calwell, and Woodson P. Welsh of company B; Capt. Harry Robinson, Lieutenants James W. Smith, and James Brazleton, of company C; Captain John C. Felton, Lieutenants Alfred A. Moore, and Emanuel D. Bass of company D.—

There were several socalled
Immune Regiments
organized among the colored people. They were supposed to be immune to yellow fever. Most of them were not needed and therefore did not see active service.

Col. Ray's regiment, from Louisiana, did splendid garrison duty in Cuba.

Major Charles Young, Third Colored Graduate from West Point Commander of the 9th Ohio Battilion.

CHAPTER XVIII.
Conclusion.

WE hope by this time the reader has seen enough of the Negro Soldier to properly appreciate his sterling worth. It might not be amiss to leave the scene of the Cuban conflict for awhile—Forget the sublime charge up San Juan Hill; turn our backs upon the thundering gates of El Saney; and relegate to the rear of memory's tablet the sickening scenes of Sibony; and lets look through the telescope of imagination, and, upon yonders lofty heights, view the colored veterans in the War of the Rebellion, when the Negro Soldiers on May the 27, 1863, were assigned the difficult task of taking Port Hudson, which to Military experts seemed almost impregnable. Situated not unlike San Juan's bushy heights, upon a high hill around, the sides and rear close under the bluff ran a bayou twelve feet deep and from fifteen to twenty feet wide. Peeping out from the openings of the embankment were the grim mouths of belching cannon.

A short rest after a long march was followed by the stern command, "Fall in." The troops were really anxious to fight and the scene reminded one more of an early athletic party than a march to death. The Confedates rediculed the idea that Negroes were to take them.

As the Negro regiment moved to-ward the fort there was a death like silence; broken only by the steady tramp of soldiers and tap of drum. "Forward, double-quick, march!" rang out along the line; guns were steady, amunition dry. but not a single piece discharged, "Right about!" was the command, the regiment wheeled to the right about three hundred yards then cooly and orderly faced the enemy again by companies.

Six awful charges were thus made when Colonel Nelson, the commander, reported to Gen. Dwight his inability to take the fort because the bayou was too deep for his men to wade; Gen. Dwight, replied "I shall consider he has accomplished nothing unless he takes those guns" Stern words those!

The soldiers, as well as Colonel Nelson, saw it was impossible to accomplish the unattainable, yet again the order to

"Charge," was obeyed with a shout, shadows of Napoleon's rugged veterans who swam the turbid waters of the Volga, and courted death under the shadows of the Pyramids of Egypt!

Color Sergeant Anselmas Planciancois (colored) said to Col. Nelson before the fight; "Colonel, I'll bring back these colors to you in honor or report to God the reason why." Subline determination! Brave Planciancois reported to God. Coporal Heath catches up the dear old colors and bears them up! up! and onward and waving defiance in a few yards of the blazing Confederate guns, he, too, lay a corpse, or rather a monument of endeavor to die and to do. Who could select a more pregnant text for a subline eulogy! History — ancient, mediaeval, and modern, shrink from the monumental task of furnishing a superior. When the days of human disinterestidness is over; when truth against error is granted an audience at the eternal bar of justice, the true historian, dipping his quill into the meteoric flash of absolute erudition, will ascribe to the Negro the first place as a brave, sacrificing and gallant soldier.

Table of Contents

Chapter I. Introductory............ 9
Chapter II. Causes Leading up to the War............................. 10
Chapter III. Negro Soldiers Enlisted in the Regular Army................ 14
Chapter IV. The 9th. Cavalry..... 20
Chapter V. The 9th's. Cuban Campaign. 24
Chapter VI. The 10th. Cavalry.... 29
Chapter VII. Some Individual Members of the 10th. 37
Chapter VIII. The 24th. Infantry.. 54
Chapter IX. The 24th. continued—the 24th. as Yellow Fever nurses... .. 69
Chapter X. In the Trenches before Santiago................................. 71
Chapter XI. The 25th. Infantry—How El Caney was won................. 77
Chapter XII. Volunteer Soldiers.. 91
Chapter XIII. The 3rd. N. C. Volunteer Infantry 105
Chapter XIV. The 8th. Illinois Volunteer Infantry 112

Chapter XV. The 23rd. Kansas Volunteer Infantry 120
Chapter XVI The 6th Va. Volunteer Infantry 139
Chapter XVII. The 10th. Georgia Volunteer Infantry; 9th. Ohio Battilion; Immune Regiments, etc. 15,
Chapter XVIII. Corciusion   16

www.ingramcontent.com/pod-product-compliance
Lightning Source LLC
Chambersburg PA
CBHW030248170426
43202CB00009B/673